A Kid's Guide
to Staying Safe Around

WATER

Maribeth Boelts

The Rosen Publishing Group's
PowerKids Press™
New York

Published in 1997 by The Rosen Publishing Group, Inc.
29 East 21st Street, New York, NY 10010

First Edition

Book Design: Erin McKenna

Photo Credits: p. 4 © Mark E. Gibson/MIDWESTOCK; p. 7 © Eric R. Berndt/MIDWESTOCK; pp. 8, 16 © Steve Ferry; p. 11 © David L. Cimino/International Stock Photography; pp. 12, 15 © Mark Gubin/MIDWESTOCK; p. 19 © Diane Guthrie/MIDWESTOCK; p. 20 © Peter Tenzer Studio, Inc./International Stock Photography.

Boelts, Maribeth.
    A kid's guide to staying safe around water / by Maribeth Boelts.
        p.   cm. — (The kids' library of personal safety)
    Includes index.
    Summary: Provides advice on how to remain safe in and around swimming pools, lakes, and oceans.
    ISBN 0-8239-5078-6 (lib. bdg.)
    1. Aquatic sports—Safety measures—Juvenile literature. [1. Aquatic sports—Safety measures. 2. Safety.] I. Title. II. Series.
    GV770.6.B64 1996
    797.2'0028'9—DC21
                                                    96-48944
                                                        CIP
                                                        AC

Manufactured in the United States of America

Contents

Swimming Is Fun

It can be fun to go swimming in a pool, in a lake, or in the blue ocean on a warm, sunny day. But do you know about water safety? There are some important rules to remember before you swim.

First, find a spot that has a **lifeguard** (LYF-gard). A lifeguard has a lot of important jobs. But the biggest job is to keep you safe while you are in the water. Is there a lifeguard in the area where you are swimming? If not, then you shouldn't go swimming.

◀ Swimming is fun, but be smart: Know the rules of water safety before you swim.

Look Before You Leap

After you know there is a lifeguard on duty, look at the water. Do you know how deep it is? Until you know how to swim well, you should swim in the **shallow** (SHAH-low) end of the pool. A grown-up can help you choose where you should swim.

If the weather looks stormy, or if it starts to rain, get out of the water right away. **Lightning** (LYT-ning) may strike in a storm, and that can be very dangerous!

Find out how deep the water ▶
is before you swim.

Swimming with a Buddy

It is not safe to swim alone. If you had trouble in the water, there would be no one to help you. Always swim with a buddy. A grown-up buddy is best. Make sure that you and your buddy swim in a place that is being watched by a lifeguard.

◀ Swimming with a buddy is the fun and safe way to swim.

Staying Safe at the Pool

The pool is a fun place to be on a hot day. But it can also be a place for trouble. Knowing the pool rules can help you stay safe. Look for a sign that lists these rules.

- Walk, don't run, on the pool deck.
- Swim in water that is not too deep.
- Don't push anyone into the pool.
- Dive only in places that are marked safe for diving.
- Don't talk to the lifeguard unless you have an **emergency** (ee-MER-jen-see). He is working hard to keep you safe.

A lifeguard's job is to keep you ▶ safe when you are swimming.

Lake Swimming

You can play some safe games in the lake wih your buddy. There is often soft sand on the bottom of the swimming area. And the water where you swim is usually shallow. If you and your buddy choose to swim in a lake, look for the lifeguard first. Next, find out how deep the water is and what is on the bottom of where you want to swim. There may be sharp or slippery stones in a certain area. Also, the water may be too shallow for jumping or diving.

◀ Swimming in a clean, clear lake can be fun.

The Ocean

The ocean is very strong. If you swim in the ocean, make sure that a grown-up is with you. Also, remember these important tips:

- Know where the lifeguard is sitting. Ask the lifeguard about the ocean **current** (KUR-ent) before you swim.
- Swim near the shore.
- Dive only when you know the area is clear.
- Watch for fish or other sea life.
- Throw away all your garbage.

The ocean is very powerful, but it can be another fun place to swim if you are careful. ▶

Life Jackets

A **life jacket** (LYF JAK-et) looks like a vest made out of balloons. It will help you float if you fall into the water. You should wear a life jacket when you are on a boat or if you are fishing. You should also wear one when the water is cold. If you fall in and if you are scared, it may be hard to swim. A life jacket can help you stay afloat until you get to safety or until someone comes to help you.

A life jacket will help if you fall into the water by accident.

Swimming Lessons

Swimming lessons are a great idea. They will help you feel safe in the water. When you feel safe, being in the water is more fun.

Lots of places offer swimming lessons. Ask your mom or dad to help you find a place where they are offered. You will learn how to hold your breath under water and float on your back. You will also learn to **tread** (TRED) water and do some basic strokes. Keep working and soon you'll be swimming well.

You will learn how to kick your legs in the water at your swimming lessons. ▶

Reach or Throw, Don't Go

If you see someone in the water who is having trouble, do not jump in the water to help her. Instead, if she is far away, you should throw something that floats to her. You can use a life jacket or a **life preserver** (LYF PRE-zerv-er). If the person is close to shore or the side of the pool, reach out to the person with something long, such as a tree branch. Keep your body low as you reach or throw. It's a good idea to shout for help, too.

◀ A life preserver can be thrown to someone who is having trouble in the water.

Be Smart and Safe

On a hot day, the cool water feels nice on your skin. But did you know that the sun can burn you even when you're in the water?

Wearing **sunscreen** (SUN-skreen) is a smart thing to do. It will help to keep your skin from getting burned. Wear it whenever you go swimming or play outside.

Swimming can be fun. But water safety tips are important to remember when you are in the water. Be a smart swimmer: Have fun and stay safe!

Glossary

current (KUR-ent) The flow of water in a certain direction.

emergency (ee-MER-jen-see) Something that comes when you don't expect it and calls for quick action.

lifeguard (LYF-gard) A person whose job is to keep people safe in the water.

life jacket (LYF JAK-et) A vest that helps you float in the water.

life preserver (LYF PRE-zerv-er) A ring or belt that floats in the water.

lightning (LYT-ning) A flash of light in the sky caused by electricity.

shallow (SHAH-low) Not deep.

sunscreen (SUN-skreen) Something that protects the skin from the sun.

tread (TRED) To move your arms and legs in the water in the same repeated motions which keeps you afloat.

Index